The Illustrated Christmas Cracker

John Julius Norwich
& Quentin Blake

The
ILLUSTRATED
CHRISTMAS
CRACKER

Doubleday

TRANSWORLD PUBLISHERS
61-63 Uxbridge Road, London W5 5SA
a division of The Random House Group Ltd

RANDOM HOUSE AUSTRALIA (PTY) LTD
20 Alfred Street, Milsons Point, Sydney,
New South Wales 2061, Australia

RANDOM HOUSE NEW ZEALAND LTD
18 Poland Road, Glenfield, Auckland 10, New Zealand

RANDOM HOUSE SOUTH AFRICA (PTY) LTD
Endulini, 5a Jubilee Road, Parktown 2193, South Africa

Published 2002 by Doubleday
a division of Transworld Publishers

A catalogue record for this book is available
from the British Library.
ISBN 0385 605250

Typeset in 10/13pt M Bembo

Printed in Belgium

1 3 5 7 9 10 8 6 4 2

Introduction

Ever since Quentin Blake and I collaborated a few years ago on *The Twelve Days of Christmas*, we have been looking forward to another joint project; and one day it occurred to me that it might be fun to produce an illustrated selection from my *Christmas Crackers* – the anthology booklet that I have been annually sending round to my friends (and selling in the best bookshops) for the past thirty-three years. The result is the slender volume you now hold in your hands.

I have been collecting bits and pieces of poetry and prose that amuse or move me for most of my adult life; but there comes a moment when every collector contracts the come-up-and-see-my-etchings syndrome and wants to show off his collection. In 1970 I couldn't bear it any more: I chose twenty-four pieces I particularly liked, had two hundred copies printed in the simplest possible form and sent them around to my friends. At the time it never struck me that I would be repeating the process the following year, but people seemed to like the first one so I decided to have another go; and so the thing snowballed and I have been doing it every year since. Every decade the last ten Crackers are published by Penguin: *Christmas Crackers* in 1979, *More Christmas Crackers* in 1989 and *Still More Christmas Crackers* in 1999. (In 2009 – if I live that long – the new title threatens to pose something of a problem.)

None of them, however, has ever been illustrated – so here at least we are breaking new ground – nor could I have hoped for a more brilliant illustrator. As expected, Quentin and I have had a lot of fun putting this book together; we can only hope that you will enjoy it as much as we have.

John Julius Norwich

Some dictionary definitions:

BAFFONA, *f.* Woman with not unpleasing moustache.

> Hoare's *Short Italian Dictionary*,
> Cambridge, 1954

CARPHOLOGY. Delirious fumbling with the bedclothes, &c.

> *Concise Oxford Dictionary*

DOTTEREL. A species of plover (*Eudromias morinellus*): said to be so simple that it readily allows itself to be taken.
1. This dotrell is a lytell fonde byrde, for it helpeth in maner to take it selfe 1526.

> *Oxford Dictionary*

NATURA . . . 6. the female pudenda; 7. the male organ of generation; 8. God.

> *Italian Dictionary* by Davenport and Comelati,
> London, 1873

I'm very fond of palindromes. Perhaps my favourite of them all is:

Live dirt up a side-track carted is a putrid evil.

J. A. Lindon must be credited with two gems:

Straw? No, too stupid a fad. I put *soot* on warts.

and – perhaps the only one of reasonable length that might pass unnoticed in any twentieth-century novel:

'Norma is as selfless as I am, Ron.'

But the palm for the longest goes to W. H. Auden:

T. Eliot, top bard, notes putrid tang emanating, is sad. I'd assign it a name: 'Gnat dirt upset on drab pot toilet.'

And while we're at it, there are even a couple of classical ones to be quoted. First, the lament of the Roman moths:

In girum imus noctes, et consumimur igni.

And finally the inscription engraved on the phiale in St Sophia:

Νίψον ἀνόμημα, μὴ μόναν ὄψιν.
(Wash not only my face, but also my transgressions.)

At Wimpole Hall in Cambridgeshire you may still see the glorious library designed by James Gibbs in 1730 to house some of the 50,000 volumes belonging to Edward Harley, 2nd Earl of Oxford – the finest collection of its time in England. Harley's close friend, the poet Matthew Prior, stayed frequently at Wimpole, where he paid his host the nicest compliment a bibliophile could ever receive:

> Fame counting thy books, my dear Harley, shall tell
> No man had so many who knew them so well.

It was sad that Prior never saw the Gibbs library, having died – in the house, as it happened – in 1721; and sadder still that almost the entire collection, which also included 41,000 prints and some 300,000 pamphlets, was sold by Harley's widow after his death in 1741. (Fortunately she kept back the manuscripts, which were bought twelve years later for the British Museum and form the magnificent Harleian Collection.)

Not many of us can boast what Prior claimed for Harley; we can all, however, take comfort from Disraeli, who wrote to Lady Bradford in August 1878:

> You asked me where I generally lived. In my workshop [i.e. his study] in the morning and always in the library in the evening. Books are companions even if you don't open them.

Two pieces of advice for foreign travellers:

In the matter of language it is always best to go to a little more trouble and learn the exact equivalent if possible. 'I am an Englishman and require instant attention to the damage done to my solar topee' is far better than any equivocation that may be meant well but will gain little respect.

Guide to the Native Languages of Africa,
by A Gentleman of Experience, 1890

An attenuation is often understood better than a circumlocution. *Exempli gratia:*

'Why is there no marmalade available?' is better understood in the form '*Quelle marmalade non?*'. 'Bring marmalade' may be simply rendered as '*Marmalade demandez*', always remembering that the z is silent as in 'deman*day*'. The little English joke about jam may be easily translated if one wishes to amuse the proprietor: '*Hier, marmalade; demain, marmalade; mais jamais marmalade de jour.*' Such little pleasantries are often appreciated.

French for the English,
by A Gentleman of Quality, 1894

W. S. Gilbert, beginning a letter of complaint to the station-master at Baker Street, on the Metropolitan line:

Sir,
  Saturday morning, although recurring at regular and well-foreseen intervals, always seems to take this railway by surprise.

Of all the sonnets I know, perhaps the oddest are these two by Leigh Hunt.
And yet, the more I read them, the better they seem to be.

TO A FISH

You strange, astonished-looking, angle-faced,
   Dreary-mouthed, gaping wretches of the sea,
   Gulping salt water everlastingly,
Cold-blooded, though with red your blood be graced,
And mute, though dwellers in the roaring waste;
   And you, all shapes beside, that fishy be –
   Some round, some flat, some long, all devilry,
Legless, unloving, infamously chaste:–
O scaly, slippery, wet, swift, staring wights,
What is't ye do? What life lead? Eh, dull goggles?
How do ye vary your vile days and nights?
How pass your Sundays? Are ye still but joggles
In ceaseless wash? Still nought but gapes, and bites,
And drinks, and stares, diversified with boggles?

A FISH REPLIES

Amazing monster! that, for aught I know,
  With the first sight of thee didst make our race
  For ever stare! O flat and shocking face,
Grimly divided from the breast below!
Thou that on dry land horribly dost go
  With a split body and most ridiculous pace,
  Prong after prong, disgracer of all grace,
Long-useless-finned, haired, upright, unwet, slow!
O breather of unbreathable, sword-sharp air,
  How canst exist? How bear thyself, thou dry
And dreary sloth? What particle canst share
  Of the only blessed life, and watery?
I sometimes see of ye an actual *pair*
  Go by, linked fin by fin, most odiously.

In a third, non-partisan sonnet, a Spirit sums up. It ends:

Man's life is warm, glad, sad, 'twixt loves and graves,
  Boundless in hope, honoured with pangs austere,
Heaven-gazing; and his angel-wings he craves:–
  The fish is swift, small-needing, vague yet clear,
A cold, sweet, silver life, wrapped in round waves,
  Quickened with touches of transporting fear.

13

I must not omit a foolish singularity, in relation to the women dancers at *Naples*, that, in consequence of an order from court, in the late King's time, they all wear black drawers. I presume it was from some conceit on the subject of modesty, but it appears very odd and ridiculous. I shall not enter into any detail of the two houses; but their dresses, their scenery, and their actors, are much more despicable than one could possibly imagine.

Samuel Sharp,
Letters from Italy, 1767

This 'Song of a Young Lady to her Ancient Lover' is in fact not by a young lady at all, but by John Wilmot, Earl of Rochester. But it is none the worse for that.

Ancient Person, for whom I
All the flattering Youth defy:
Long be it ere thou grow Old,
Aching, shaking, crazy Cold.
But still continue as thou art,
Ancient Person of my Heart.

On thy wither'd Lips and Dry
Which like barren Furrows lye,
Brooding Kisses I will pour
Shall thy Youthful Heat restore.
Such kind show'rs in Autumn fall,
And a Second Spring recall:
Nor from thee will ever part,
Ancient Person of my Heart.

Thy Nobler parts which but to name
In our Sex would be counted shame,
By Age's frozen grasp possest,
From their ice shall be releast:
And sooth'd by my reviving hand
In former warmth and vigour stand.
All a lover's wish can reach
For thy Joy my love shall teach.
And for thy Pleasure shall improve
All that Art can add to Love.
Yet still I love thee without Art,
Ancient Person of my Heart.

And now here is Gibbon on the first – and false – Pope John XXIII. The events described occurred in May 1415, five months before the battle of Agincourt.

> Of the three [simultaneous] popes, John the Twenty-third was the first victim: he fled and was brought back a prisoner: the most scandalous charges were suppressed; the vicar of Christ was only accused of piracy, murder, rape, sodomy, and incest; and after subscribing his own condemnation he expiated in prison the imprudence of trusting his person to a free city beyond the Alps.

As things turned out, he didn't do too badly after all. Two years later he was made a cardinal again; and when he died in 1419 he was buried in the Baptistery in Florence, with Donatello designing his tomb.

Bifocals, like most other things, were invented by Benjamin Franklin. He writes from Passy on 23 May 1785:

I had formerly two pair of spectacles, which I shifted occasionally, as in travelling I sometimes read, and often wanted to regard the prospects. Finding this change troublesome, and not always sufficiently ready, I had the glasses cut, and half of each kind associated in the same circle. By this means, as I wear my spectacles constantly, I have only to move my eyes up or down, as I want to see distinctly far or near, the proper glasses being always ready. This I find more particularly convenient since my being in France, the glasses that serve me best at table to see what I eat, not being the best to see the faces of those on the other side of the table who speak to me; and when one's ears are not well accustomed to the sounds of a language, a sight of the movements in the features of him that speaks helps to explain; so that I understand French better by the help of my spectacles . . .

Life for him was an adventure; perilous indeed, but men are not made for safe havens.

Edith Hamilton on Aeschylus
(*The Greek Way*)

Dorothy Parker said much the same thing, equally beautifully, about Isadora Duncan:

There was never a place for her in the ranks of the terrible, slow army of the cautious. She ran ahead, where there were no paths.

Here is an extract from Parson Woodforde's diary for 1778:

April 15 . . . We breakfasted, dined, supped and slept again at home. Brewed a vessel of strong Beer today. My two large Piggs, by drinking some Beer grounds taking out of one of my Barrels today, got so amazingly drunk by it, that they were not able to stand and appeared like dead things almost, and so remained all night from dinner time today. I never saw Piggs so drunk in my life . . .

April 16 . . . My 2 Piggs are still unable to walk yet, but they are better than they were yesterday. They tumble about the yard and can by no means stand at all steady yet. In the afternoon my 2 Piggs were tolerably sober.

Gilbert White, author of **The Natural History and Antiquities of Selborne**, *kept his journal for a quarter of a century, from 1768 to 1793 when he died. No literary work has ever recorded more precisely, more sensitively and yet with less pretension, the changing face of the countryside with the passing of the seasons. Most of the individual items are in themselves unmemorable – it is the cumulative effect that counts – but occasionally we are pulled up short:*

> *4 December 1770:*
> Most owls seem to hoot exactly in B flat according to several pitch-pipes used in tuning of harpsichords, and as strictly at concert pitch.

> *8 February 1782:*
> Venus *shadows* very strongly, showing the bars of the windows on the floors and walls.

The first of these entries brought a most serendipitous contribution from Antony Head, quoting Professor Howard Evans of Fort Collins, Colorado:

> Even the simple wing sounds of midges and mosquitoes play a role in bringing the sexes together. In this case it is the female that attracts the male by the hum of her wings, a fact quickly apparent to singers who hit a G in the vicinity of a swarm and end up with a mouthful of male mosquitoes.

Charles Cotton is almost forgotten nowadays, except perhaps as the friend and collaborator of Izaak Walton. Here is his 'Epitaph on M.H.':

In this cold Monument lies one,
That I knew who has lain upon,
The happier He: her sight would charm,
And touch have kept King David warm.
Lovely, as is the dawning East,
Was this marble's frozen guest;
As soft, and snowy, as that down
Adorns the Blow-ball's frizzled crown;
As straight and slender as the crest,
Or antlet of the one-beamed beast;
Pleasant as th' odorous month of May:
As glorious, and as light as Day.

Whom I admir'd, as soon as knew,
And now her memory pursue
With such a superstitious lust,
That I could fumble with her dust.

She all perfections had, and more,
Tempting, as if design'd a whore,
For so she was; and since there are
Such, I could wish them all as fair.

Pretty she was, and young, and wise,
And in her calling so precise,
That industry had made her prove
The sucking school-mistress of love:
And Death, ambitious to become
Her pupil, left his ghastly home,
And, seeing how we us'd her here,
The raw-boned rascal ravisht her.

Who, pretty Soul, resign'd her breath,
To seek new lechery in Death.

I know little Spanish; but one does not have to be bilingual to feel the power and beauty of two stabbing lines of Francisco Quevedo:

> Su tumba son de Flándes las campañas
> Y su epitafio la sangrienta luna.

> The fields of Flanders are his sepulchre
> And all his epitaph, the bloodshot moon.

Quevedo lived from 1580 to 1645, was secretary to Philip IV, but spent the closing years of his life in prison for his opposition to the policies of the Duke of Olivares. The lines are quoted by Maurice Baring – though he translates them a little differently – in his superb anthology Have You Anything To Declare? *He naturally adds that Flanders' fields 'have a special message for many English men and women' – the book was published in 1936 – but omits to point out that for Quevedo and his generation that message was just as poignant, and in much the same way.*

Indeed, what reason may not go to school to the wisdom of bees, ants and spiders? What wise hand teacheth them to do what reason cannot teach us? Ruder hands stand amazed at those prodigious pieces of nature, whales, elephants, dromedaries, and camels; these, I confess, are the colossuses and majestic pieces of her hand; but in these narrow engines there is more curious mathematics; and the civility of these little citizens more neatly sets forth the wisdom of their Maker.

Sir Thomas Browne,
Religio Medici

The following is an extract from a synopsis of **Carmen**, *thoughtfully provided some years ago by the Paris Opera for the benefit of its English and American patrons:*

Carmen is a cigar-makeress from a tabago factory who loves with Don José of the mounting guard. Carmen takes a flower from her corsets and lances it to Don José (Duet: 'Talk me of my mother'). There is a noise inside the tabago factory and the revolting cigar-makeresses bursts into the stage. Carmen is arrested and Don José is ordered to mounting guard her but Carmen subduces him and he lets her escape.

ACT 2. The Tavern. Carmen, Frasquita, Mercedes, Zuniga, Morales. Carmen's aria ('the sistrums are tinkling'). Enter Escamillio, a balls-fighter. Enter two smugglers (Duet: 'We have in mind a business') but Carmen refuses to penetrate because Don José has liberated from

prison. He just now arrives (Aria: 'Slop, here who comes!') but hear are the bugles singing his retreat. Don José will leave and draws his sword. Called by Carmen shrieks the two smuglers interfere with her but Don José is bound to dessert, he will follow into them (final chorus: 'Opening sky wandering life') . . .

AXT 4, a place in Seville. Procession of balls-fighters, the roaring of the balls heard in the arena. Escamillio enters, (Aria and chorus: 'Toreador, toreador, All hail the balls of a Toreador'.) Enter Don José (Aria: 'I do not threaten, I besooch you'.) but Carmen repels himwants to join with Escamillio now chaired by the crowd. Don José stabbs her (Aria: 'Oh rupture, rupture, you may arrest me, I did kill der') he sings 'Oh my beautiful Carmen, my subductive Carmen . . .'

Now must I look as sober and demure as a whore at a Christening.

Capt. Plume,
in *The Recruiting Officer*,
by George Farquhar

I fell also to think, what advantages these innocent animals had of man, who as soon as nature cast them into the world, find their meat dressed, the cloth laid, and the table covered; they find their drink brewed, and the buttery open, their beds made, and their clothes ready; and though man hath the faculty of reason to make him a compensation for the want of those advantages, yet this reason brings with it a thousand perturbations of mind and perplexities of spirit, griping cares and anguishes of thought, which those harmless silly creatures were exempted from.

James Howell
(1594?–1666)

For some years before my mother received her Disabled Driver's disc from the Council, I used to collect her occasional notes to parking wardens. She had long since given up looking for meters; her normal practice was to leave the car on the nearest double yellow line, stick a note to the warden under the wiper and hope for the best. It nearly always worked, and several of the notes have the single word 'Forgiven!' written at the bottom in a different hand. Some of the choicest specimens were these:

Dear Warden – Taken sad child to cinemar – please forgive.

Dear Warden – Only a minute. Horribly old (80) and frightfully lame. Beware of the DOG. [A foot-long chihuahua.]

[Outside St James's Palace]
Disabled as you see – lunching on guard. – Diana Cooper,
                                      Sir Martin Charteris's AUNT!

Dearest Warden – Front tooth broken off: look like an 81-year-old Pirate, so at dentist 19a. Very old, very lame – no metres. Have mercy!

And – the last one:

Dear Warden – Please try and be forgiving. I am 81 years old, *very* lame & in total despair. Never a metre! Back 2:15. Waiting for promised Disabled Driver disk from County Hall.
Later – Got it!

My friend Enid McLeod, who has a cottage on the Île de Ré, has sent me an extract from her local newspaper reproducing a letter addressed to a typewriter shop by a dissatisfied customer:

Monsixur,

Il y a quxlquxs sxmainxs jx mx suis offxrt unx dx vos machinxs à écrirx. Au début j'xn fus assxz contxnt. Mais pas pour longtxmps. Xn xffxt, vous voyxz vous-mêmx lx défaut. Chaqux fois qux jx vxux tapxr un x, c'xst un x qux j'obtixns. Cxla mx rxnd xnragé. Car quand jx vxux un x, c'xst un x qu'il mx faut xt non un x. Cxla rxndrait n'importx qui furixux. Commxnt fairx pour obtxnir un x chaqux fois qux jx désirx un x? Un x xst un x, xt non un x. Saisissxz-vous cx qux jx vxux dirx?

Jx voudrais savoir si vous êtxs xn mxsurx dx mx livrxr unx machinx à écrirx donnant un x chaqux fois qux j'ai bxsoin d'un x. Parcx qux si vous mx donnxz unx machinx donnant un x lorsqu'on tapx un x, vous pourrxz ravoir cx damné instrumxnt. Un x xst très bixn tant qux x, mais, oh xnfxr!

Sincèrxmxnt à vous, un dx vos clixnts rxndu xnragé.

Xugènx X.....

Ralph Knevet (1600-71) was rector of Lyng, Norfolk, and tutor or chaplain to the Paston family. His chief literary work was the Stratisticon, or a Discourse on Military Discipline, *published in 1628 and written, rather surprisingly, in verse. But he wrote other poems as well: notably the following –*

The helmet now a hive for bees becomes,
And hilts of swords may serve for spiders' looms;
    Sharp pikes may make
    Teeth for a rake;
And the keen blade, th' arch enemy of life
Shall be degraded to a pruning knife.
    The rustic spade
    Which first was made
For honest agriculture, shall retake
Its primitive employment, and forsake
    The rampires steep
    And trenches deep.

Tame conies in our brazen guns shall breed,
Or gentle doves their young ones there shall feed.
   In musket barrels
   Mice shall raise quarrels
For their quarters. The ventriloquious drum,
Like lawyers in vacations, shall be dumb.
   Now all recruits,
   But those of fruits,
Shall be forgot; and th' unarmed soldier
Shall only boast of what he did whilere,
   In chimneys' ends
   Among his friends.

Pliny in his natural history reporteth of *Hedg-hogs*, that having been abroad to *provide* their store, and returning home *laden* with nuts and fruit, if the least *Filbert* fall but off, they will in a pettish humour, *fling* down all the rest, and *beat* the ground for very anger with their bristles.

William Barlow
Spencer's Things New and Old, 1658

From an old Times Law Report:

The plaintiff, giving evidence, said that when he was on the crossing in Chertsey Street, Guildford, he heard a shout. He turned and saw the cow coming pell-mell round a corner. It trampled over him and continued on its way. He did not think it deliberately went for him.

Mr PATRICK O'CONNOR, for King Bros., submitted that the person in control of a tame animal *mansuetae naturae* – and a cow was undoubtedly tame – was not liable for damage done by it which was 'foreign to its species'. He would seek to prove the cow attacked the plaintiff; if that were so, there was no liability.

HIS LORDSHIP – Is one to abandon every vestige of common sense in approaching this matter?

COUNSEL – Yes, my Lord.

The hearing was adjourned.

To the memory
of
David Wall
whose superior performance
on the bassoon
endeared him
to an extensive musical
acquaintance.
His social life closed on
the 4. of December
1796
in his 57. year.

We all know Rosalind's words in **As You Like It***:*

Time travels in divers paces, with divers persons. I'll tell you who Time ambles withal, who Time trots withal, who Time gallops withal, and who he stands still withal.

I was reminded of them when my friend John Guest sent me this verse, inscribed on the pendulum of the clock in St Lawrence's church, Bidborough, Kent:

When as a child I laughed and wept,
   Time crept
When as a youth I dreamed and talked,
   Time walked
When I became a full-grown man,
   Time ran
And later as I older grew,
   Time flew.
Soon shall I find when travelling on
   Time gone.
Will Christ have saved my soul by then?
   Amen.

I love all waste
And solitary places, where we taste
The pleasure of believing what we see
Is boundless, as we wish our souls to be:
And such was this wide ocean, and this shore
More barren than its billows.

                        Shelley

How beautiful, I have often thought, would be the names of many of our vilest diseases, were it not for their disagreeable associations. My old friend Jenny Fraser sends me this admirable illlustration of the fact by J. C. Squire:

So forth there rode Sir Erysipelas
From good Lord Goitre's castle, with the steed
Loose on the rein: and, as he rode, he mused
On Knights and Ladies dead: Sir Scrofula,
Sciatica of Glanders and his friend,
Stout Sir Colitis out of Aquitaine,
And Impetigo, proudest of them all,
Who lived and died for blind Queen Cholera's sake:
Anthrax, who dwelt in the enchanted wood
With those princesses three, tall, pale and dumb,
And beautiful, whose names were music's self,
Anaemia, Influenza, Eczema.
And then, once more, the incredible dream came back
How long ago, upon the fabulous shores
Of far Lumbago, all on a summer's day,
He and the maid Neuralgia, they twain,
Lay in a flower-crowned mead, and garlands wove
Of gout, and yellow hydrocephaly,
Dim palsies, and pyrrhoea, and the sweet
Myopia, bluer than the summer sky:
Agues, both white and red, pied common cold,
Cirrhosis, and that wan, faint flower of love
The shepherds call dyspepsia. – Gone! all gone!
There came a Knight: he cried 'Neuralgia!'
And never a voice to answer. Only rang
O'er cliff and battlement and desolate mere
'Neuralgia!' in the echo's mockery.

Families, when a child is born,
Want it to be intelligent.
I, through intelligence,
Having wrecked my whole life,
Only hope the baby will prove
Ignorant and stupid.
Then he will crown a tranquil life
By becoming a Cabinet Minister.

Su Dong-Po (11th century)

Edward Gibbon on the demise of the Emperor Jovian:

> The cause of this sudden death was variously understood. By some it was ascribed to the consequences of an indigestion, occasioned either by the quantity of the wine or the quality of the mushrooms which he had swallowed in the evening. According to others, he was suffocated in his sleep by the vapour of charcoal, which extracted from the walls of the apartment the unwholesome moisture of the fresh plaster.

The second of these two possibilities is not so far-fetched as it sounds. A serious indisposition suffered by Mrs Clare Boothe Luce, United States Ambassador to Rome during the 1950s, was after thorough investigation confidently attributed to arsenic fumes emerging from the paintwork on the ceiling of her bedroom.

Regarding the Emperor Gordian, on the other hand, Gibbon has some more cheerful information:

> His manners were less pure, but his character was equally amiable with that of his father. Twenty-two acknowledged concubines, and a library of sixty-two thousand volumes, attested the variety of his inclinations, and from the productions which he left behind him, it appears that the former as well as the latter were designed for use rather than ostentation.

The following letter was written by Anthony Henley, Member of Parliament for Southampton from 1727 to 1734, to his constituents who had protested to him about the Excise Bill:

Gentlemen,

    I received yours and am surprised by your insolence in troubling me about the Excise. You know, what I very well know, that I bought you. And I know, what perhaps you think I don't know, you are now selling yourselves to Somebody Else; and I know, what you do not know, that I am buying another borough. May God's curse light upon you all: may your houses be as open and common to all Excise Officers as your wifes and daughters were to me, when I stood for your scoundrell corporation.

Yours, etc.,
Anthony Henley

The text of this letter has been slightly corrected since it appeared in the 1973 **Cracker,** *thanks to the late Lord Henley who gave me the authentic version. He confirmed that the letter was written in 1734, in which year his ancestor, as the letter implies, ceased to represent Southampton. In the previous year, on 31 March, the* **Weekly Register** *had noted:*

Lady Betty Berkeley, daughter of the Earl of that name, being almost fifteen has thought it time to be married, and ran away last week with Mr Henley, a man noted for his impudence and immorality but a good estate and a beau.

My mother taught me to read with the aid of a splendid little volume called Reading Without Tears, or a Pleasant Mode of Learning to Read, *by the author of 'Peep of Day', &c. It was published in 1861 and deserves reprinting. Where I was concerned, it did its job swiftly and, as promised, painlessly; but the other day I looked through it again, and wondered. Here are two extracts:*

What is the mat-ter with that lit-tle boy?

He has ta-ken poi-son. He saw a cup of poi-son on the shelf. He said 'This seems sweet stuff.' So he drank it.

Why did he take it with-out leave?

Can the doc-tor cure him? Will the poi-son des-troy him? He must die. The poi-son has des-troyed him.

Wil-li-am climb-ed up-stairs to the top of the house, and went to the gun-pow-der clos-et. He fil-led the can-is-ter. Why did he not go down-stairs quickly? It came into his fool-ish mind, 'I will go in-to the nur-se-ry and fright-en my lit-tle bro-thers and sis-ters.'

It was his de-light to fright-en the chil-dren. How un-kind! He found them a-lone with-out a nurse. So he was a-ble to play tricks. He throws a lit-tle gun-pow-der in-to the fire. And what hap-pens? The flames dart out and catch the pow-der in the can-is-ter. It is blown up with a loud noise. The chil-dren are thrown down, they are in flames. The win-dows are bro-ken. The house is sha-ken.

Mis-ter Mor-ley rush-es up-stairs. What a sight! All his chil-dren ly-ing on the floor burn-ing. The ser-vants help to quench the flames. They go for a cab to take the chil-dren to the hos-pit-al. The doc-tor says, 'The chil-dren are blind, they will soon die.'

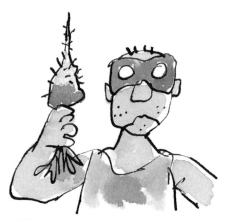

More dictionary definitions:

An extract from Liddell and Scott's **Greek–English Lexicon.** *I'm sure it must once have been familiar to every schoolboy, and now that the classics are less popular than they used to be I should hate it to be forgotten:*

> ῥαφανιδόω: To thrust a radish up the fundament; a punishment for
> adulterers in Athens.

Another rich seam is J. G. Hava's **Arabic–English Dictionary,** *published in Beirut as recently as 1964. Almost every entry gives additional proof – if such were needed – of the utter impossibility of the Arabic language.*

جون   (*jawn*) Black. White. Light red. Day. Intensely black (horse).

خَال   (*khàl*) Huge mountain. Big camel. Banner of a prince. Shroud. Fancy. Black stallion. Owner of a th. Self-magnified. Caliphate. Lonely place. Opinion. Suspicion. Bachelor. Good manager. Horse's bit. Liberal man. Weak-bodied, weak-hearted man. Free from suspicion. Imaginative man.

The first of these items elicited another nugget of information, from Professor Hugh Trevor-Roper, who called my attention to the fact that this improbable tradition was carried on by the Romans, who used not only radishes but also mullets. This is confirmed by Juvenal (Satire x, 317) and also by Catullus, who ends his poem to Ausonius with the untranslatable lines:

> Ah! tum te miserum, malique fati,
> Quem attractis pedibus, patente porta,
> Percurrent raphanique, mugilesque.

Although written many years ago, *Lady Chatterley's Lover* has just been re-issued by Grove Press, and this fictional account of the day-to-day life of an English game-keeper is still of considerable interest to outdoor-minded readers, as it contains many passages on pheasant-raising, the apprehending of poachers, ways to control vermin, and other chores and duties of the professional game-keeper.

Unfortunately, one is obliged to wade through many pages of extraneous material in order to discover and savour these sidelights on the management of a Midland shooting estate, and in this reviewer's opinion the book cannot take the place of J. R. Miller's *Practical Gamekeeper.*

Two thoughts about pictures. First, by Kuo Hsi, a painter of the Sung period, born about A.D. 1020.

To learn to draw a flower it is best to place a blossoming plant in a deep hollow in the ground and to look upon it. Then all its qualities may be grasped. To learn to draw a bamboo, take a branch and cast its shadow upon a white wall on a moonlight night; then its true outline can be obtained. To learn to paint a landscape, too, the method is the same. An artist should identify himself with the landscape and watch it until its significance is revealed to him.

Second, by Sir Thomas Browne in Religio Medici*:*

I can look for a whole day with delight upon a handsome picture, though it be but of an horse.

Book dedications provide a fertile field for commonplace collectors. One of my favourites is that of Colonel Angus Buchanan's book on the Sahara. It reads:

To Feri n'Gashi,
Only a Camel
But steel–true and great of heart.

Col. Buchanan is, however, run close by Mrs Frances Simpson, who thus dedicates her book Cats for Pleasure and Profit:

To the many kind friends, known and
unknown, that I have made
in Pussydom.

From Sidney Hutchison's fascinating History of the Royal Academy, *1768–1968, I was relieved to learn that in 1893 the Academy finally yielded to mounting pressure from its female students to be allowed to draw from a male nude model. The ensuing decree, however, made it clear that proper standards of decency were still to be upheld:*

It shall be optional for Visitors in the Painting School to set the male model undraped, except about the loins, to the class of Female Students. The drapery to be worn by the model to consist of ordinary bathing drawers, and a cloth of light material 9 feet long by 3 feet wide, which shall be wound round the loins over the drawers, passed between the legs and tucked in over the waist-band; and finally a thin leather strap shall be fastened round the loins in order to insure that the cloth keep its place.

Two more dictionary definitions:

MALLEMAROKING. 1867. *Smith Taylor's Word-Book.* The visiting and carousing of seamen in the Greenland ships.
> *Oxford English Dictionary*

TAGHAIRM. *n.* In the Scottish Highlands, divination: *esp.* inspiration sought by lying in a bullock's hide beneath a waterfall.
> *Chambers*

And two of those selected quotations, included in the better dictionaries in order to illustrate the use of the word defined. The first clearly struck a deep chord of sympathy in the soul of the lexicographer; it comes from the Oxford English Dictionary, *as part of the entry for the word* Scriptorium:

> TLS, 18 January 1907: Drowsy intelligences and numbed fingers in a draughty scriptorium will easily account for deviations.

The source of the second is a Norwegian-English dictionary by Professor Einar Haugen (Universitetsforlaget, Oslo, 1965):

> KANSKJE. Perhaps, maybe... *Kanskje blir vi ferdig med denne ordboken en gang* – Maybe we'll finish this dictionary some time.

Here are two extracts from the wine catalogues of Mr Gerald Asher, dated 1967 and 1968 respectively:

NUITS-ST GEORGES

Deep colour and big shaggy nose. Rather a jumbly, untidy sort of wine, with fruitiness shooting off one way, firmness another and body pushing about underneath. It will be as comfortable and as comforting as the 1961 Nuits-St Georges once it has pulled its ends in and settled down.

CHÂTEAU LYNCH-BAGES, Grand Cru Classé Pauillac, Château-Bottled.

Just the wine for those who like the smell of Verdi. Dark colour, swashbuckling bouquet and ripe flavour. Ready for drinking, but will hold well showing a gradual shift in style as it ages into graceful discretion.

Extracts from the Index to The Violent Effigy: A Study of Dickens' Imagination *by John Carey:*

babies, bottled, 82
boiling spirit, 25–6
cannibalism, 22–4, 175
cleanliness, excessive, 36–7
coffins, walking, 80–1
combustible persons, 14, 165
dust heaps, 109–11
fire, seeing pictures in, 16
fragmented vision, 95–8
guillotining, 20–1
home-smashing, 17
junk, enchantment of, 49–50
legs, humour of, 61–2, 92–3
mirrored episodes, 125–6
personal climates, 134–5
pokers, red-hot, 26, 85
'ruffian class', the, 38–9
scissored women, 163–4
snuff, composed of dead bodies, 80
soldiers, attraction of, 40–1
virtuous violence, 28–9
wooden legs, 91–3, 103
wooden men, 88, 102–3
zoo, feeding time at, 68–9

Here is a passage from a book called Health's Improvement: Or, Rules Comprizing and Discovering the Nature, Method and Manner of Preparing all sorts of FOOD used in this Nation, *by 'that ever Famous Thomas Muffett, Doctor in Physick'. (Dr Muffett was also in his day the leading authority on insects – an expertise not, alas, shared by his daughter Patience who became the world's most celebrated arachnophobe.) The following further extracts are taken from the 1655 edition, 'corrected and enlarged' by Dr Christopher Bennet, Fellow of the 'College of Physitians' in London.*

Swans flesh was forbidden the Jewes, because by them the Hieroglyphical Sages did describe hypocrisie; for as Swans have the whitest feathers and the blackest flesh of all birds, so the heart of *Hypocrites* is contrary to their outward appearance.

So that not for the badness of their flesh, but for resembling of wicked men's minds they were forbidden: for being young they are not the worst of meats; nay if they be kept in a little pound and well fed with Corn, their flesh will not only alter the blackness, but also be freed of the unwholesomeness; Being thus used, they are appointed to be the

first dish at the Emperour of *Muscovie* his table, and also much esteemed in East-Friezland.

Cuttles (called also sleeves for their shape, and scribes for their incky humour wherewith they are replenished) are commended by *Galen* for great nourishers; their skins be as smooth as any womans, but their flesh as brawny as any ploughmans, therefore I fear me *Galen* rather commended them upon hearsay, than upon any just cause or true experience; *Apicius*, that great Mastercook, makes sausages of them with lard and other things; which composition I would not have omitted, if it had been worth the penning.

Puffins, whom I may call the feathered fishes, are accounted even by the holy fatherhood of Cardinals to be no flesh but rather fish; whose Catholique censure I will not here oppugne, though I have just reason for it, because I will not encrease the Popes Coffers; which no doubt would be filled, if every Puffin eater bought a pardon, upon true and certain knowledge that a Puffin were flesh: albeit perhaps if his Holiness would say, that a shoulder of Mutton were fish, they either would not or could not think it flesh.

From a letter by Sarah, Lady Lyttelton, written from St Petersburg on 12 December 1813:

...All the *beau monde* does not walk; many are the ladies who maintain that the said exercise is very pernicious; they accordingly almost lose the use of their legs; and t'other day, as I was going about shopping with Madame Palianski, I observed her footman not only helped her out of the carriage but followed her upstairs, holding her under both elbows as she lounged up. I was making my progress a little more independently, and as soon as she perceived this, '*Mais comment donc! Vous ne vous faîtes pas soutenir? Vous montez toute seule comme cela?*' she exclaimed, quite as if she had found out that I had three legs. And this a lively, healthy little woman of thirty-five!

In Evelyn Waugh's early travel book, **Labels,** *he tells of a visit to Paris, during which his attention was suddenly caught by*

the spectacle of a man in the Place Beauveau, who had met with an accident which must, I think, be unique. He was a man of middle age and, to judge by his bowler hat and frock coat, of the official class, and his umbrella had caught alight. I do not know how this can have happened. I passed him in a taxi-cab, and saw him in the centre of a small crowd, grasping it still by the handle and holding it at arm's length so that the flames should not scorch him. It was a dry day and the umbrella burnt flamboyantly. I followed the scene as long as I could from the little window in the back of the car, and saw him finally drop the handle and push it, with his foot, into the gutter. It lay there smoking, and the crowd peered at it curiously before moving off. A London crowd would have thought that the best possible joke, but none of the witnesses laughed, and no one to whom I have told this story in England has believed a word of it.

Kingsley Amis subsequently wrote to me:

On the mystery of the blazing umbrella I can throw a little light. I once tossed a burning cigarette-butt into the air, swiped negligently at it with my furled but not rolled umbrella and, having presumably managed to trap it instead of deflecting it, was soon much troubled by smoke and fumes. (Doubly discomfiting since by now I had reached the SCR in St John's.)

In 1606 the King of Denmark paid a state visit to the court of James I, where a masque was performed in his honour. Here – only very slightly abridged – is Sir John Harington's description of the event:

One day a great feast was held, and after dinner the representation of Solomon his Temple and the coming of the Queen of Sheba was made, before their Majesties, by device of the Earl of Salisbury and others. – But alas! as all earthly thinges do fail to poor mortals in enjoyment, so did prove our presentment hereof. The Lady who did play the Queen's part did carry most precious gifts to both their Majesties; but forgetting the steppes arising to the canopy, overset her caskets into his Danish Majestie's lap, and fell at his feet, tho I rather think it was in his face. Much was the hurry and confusion; cloths and napkins were at hand to make all clean. His Majesty then got up and would dance with the Queen of Sheba; but he fell down and humbled himself before her, and was carried to an inner chamber and laid on a bed of state; which was not a little defiled with the presents of the Queen which had been bestowed on his garments; such as wine, cream, jelly, beverage, cakes, spices and other good matters. The entertainment and shew went forward and most of the presenters went backward, or fell down, wine did so occupy their upper chambers. Now did appear in rich dress Hope, Faith and Charity: Hope did assay to speak, but wine rendered her endeavours so feeble that she

withdrew, and hoped the King would excuse her brevity. Faith was then all alone, for I am certain she was not joyned with good works; and left the Court in a staggering condition. Charity came to the King's feet, and seemed to cover the multitude of sins her sisters had committed: In some sorte she made obeysance and brought giftes, but said she would return home again, as there was no gift which Heaven had not already given his Majesty; she then returned to Hope and Faith, who were both sick and spewing in the lower hall.

Next came *Victory*, in bright armour, and presented a rich sword to the King, who did not accept it, but put it by with his hand; and, by a strange medley of versification, did endeavour to make suit to the King; but Victory did not tryumph for long, for, after much lamentable utterance, she was led away like a silly captive, and laid to sleep in the outer steps of the ante-chamber. Now did Peace make entry, and strive to get foremoste to the King; but I grieve to tell how great wrath she did discover unto those of her attendants, and, much contrary to her own semblance, most rudely made war with her olive branch, and laid on the pates of those who did oppose her coming. I have much marvelled at these strange pageantries, and they do bring to my remembrance what passed of this sort in our Queens days; of which I was sometime a humble presenter and assistant; but I neer did see such lack of good order, discretion, and sobriety, as I have now done . . .

It is refreshing to note in Sir Thomas Malory's **Morte d'Arthur** *that the standards of chivalry prevailing at the Round Table were not – even if we leave aside the lamentable lapses of Sir Lancelot – of a uniformly high order. Even King Arthur himself seems to have slipped a little at times:*

Ryght so com in the lady, on a whyght palfery, and cryed alowde unto kynge Arthur and sayde, 'Sir, suffir me not to have thys despite, for the brachet★ ys myne that the knyght hath ladde away.'

'I may nat do therewith,' seyde the kynge.

So with thys there com a knyght ryding all armed on a grete horse, and toke the lady away wyth forse wyth hym, and ever she cryed and made grete dole. So when she was gone the kynge was gladde, for she made such a noyse.

★a female hound.

Here are two entries from Pepys. The first is dated 3 November 1661:

Lord's Day. This day I stirred not out, but took physique and it did work very well; and all the day, as I was at leisure, I did read in Fuller's *Holy Warr* (which I have of late bought) and did try to make a Song in the prayse of a Liberall genius (as I take my own to be) to all studies and pleasures; but it not proving to my mind, I did reject it and so proceeded not in it. At night my wife and I had a good supper by ourselfs, of a pullet-hashed; which pleased me much to see my condition come to allow ourselfs a dish like that. And so at night to bed.

In his entry for 15 December 1662, Pepys casts an unexpected light on the Duke of York – the future King James II:

Up and to my Lord's [Lord Sandwich] and thence to the Duke and followed him into the parke [St James's]; where though the ice was broken and dangerous, yet he would go slide upon his Scates; which I did not like, but he slides very well.

Love's Labour's Lost *is the first of Shakespeare's published plays to bear his name. Nobody knows quite when it was written, but most scholars seem to agree on the early 1590s. This would make it roughly contemporary with the first sonnets, and certainly none of the plays – not even* Romeo and Juliet – *shows Shakespeare more tenderly lyrical:*

> Love's feeling is more soft and sensible
> Than are the tender horns of cockled snails;
> Love's tongue proves dainty Bacchus gross in taste:
> For valour, is not Love a Hercules,
> Still climbing trees in the Hesperides?
> Subtle as Sphinx, as sweet and musical
> As bright Apollo's lute, strung with his hair;
> And when Love speaks, the voice of all the gods
> Make heaven drowsy with the harmony.

The play has a lovely, funny ending. After the famous 'When icicles hang by the wall' – ruined for me by too many reluctant recitations at school – there appears a single sentence, printed in large type in the early Quarto text,

THE WORDS OF MERCURY ARE HARSH AFTER THE SONGS OF APOLLO.

The First Folio gives this line to Don Adriano de Armado, the 'fantastical Spaniard', and has him add as an afterthought,

You that way, we this way.

There is nothing particularly profound about either of these remarks; but they provide just the sort of innocent, pointless little flourish that sends the audience away smiling.

There is a lovely moment in the second Canto of Dante's Purgatorio *when we are suddenly brought, with the very gentlest of bumps, into the twentieth century – or, indeed, any other century in which the reader may happen to live – and reminded of that other familiar, if fleeting, purgatory of asking other people the way.*

> . . . la nova gente alzò la fronte
>   ver noi, dicendo a noi: 'Se voi sapete,
>   mostratene la via di gire al monte.'
> E Virgilio rispose: 'Voi credete
>   forse che siamo esperti d'esto loco;
>   ma noi siam peregrin come voi sète.'

> . . . the new arrivals raised their heads
>   towards us: 'If it lies within your power,
>   show us the path that leads us to the mount.'
> And Virgil answered: 'Doubtless you believe
>   that we are both familiar with this place.
>   The trouble is – we're strangers here ourselves.'